Title: DragonFlies
R.L.: 1 9
PTS:
TST:

D1544584

INSECTS UP CLOSE

Dragonflies

by Patrick Perish

BLASTOFF! READERS

BELLWETHER MEDIA · MINNEAPOLIS, MN

Note to Librarians, Teachers, and Parents:

Blastoff! Readers are carefully developed by literacy experts and combine standards-based content with developmentally appropriate text.

Level 1 provides the most support through repetition of high-frequency words, light text, predictable sentence patterns, and strong visual support.

Level 2 offers early readers a bit more challenge through varied simple sentences, increased text load, and less repetition of high-frequency words.

Level 3 advances early-fluent readers toward fluency through increased text and concept load, less reliance on visuals, longer sentences, and more literary language.

Level 4 builds reading stamina by providing more text per page, increased use of punctuation, greater variation in sentence patterns, and increasingly challenging vocabulary.

Level 5 encourages children to move from "learning to read" to "reading to learn" by providing even more text, varied writing styles, and less familiar topics.

Whichever book is right for your reader, Blastoff! Readers are the perfect books to build confidence and encourage a love of reading that will last a lifetime!

This edition first published in 2018 by Bellwether Media, Inc.

No part of this publication may be reproduced in whole or in part without written permission of the publisher. For information regarding permission, write to Bellwether Media, Inc., Attention: Permissions Department, 5357 Penn Avenue South, Minneapolis, MN 55419.

Library of Congress Cataloging-in-Publication Data

Names: Perish, Patrick.
Title: Dragonflies / by Patrick Perish.
Description: Minneapolis, MN : Bellwether Media, Inc., 2018. | Series:
    Blastoff! Readers. Insects Up Close | Audience: Ages 5-8. | Audience: K to
    grade 3. | Includes bibliographical references and index.
Identifiers: LCCN 2016055082 (print) | LCCN 2017006495 (ebook) | ISBN
    9781626176621 (hardcover : alk. paper) | ISBN 9781681033921 (ebook)
Subjects: LCSH: Dragonflies–Juvenile literature.
Classification: LCC QL520 .P47 2018 (print) | LCC QL520 (ebook) | DDC
    595.7/33–dc23
LC record available at https://lccn.loc.gov/2016055082

Editor: Christina Leighton   Designer: Jon Eppard

Printed in the United States of America, North Mankato, MN.

Table of Contents

What Are Dragonflies?

Dragonflies are powerful fliers. These insects zip through the air!

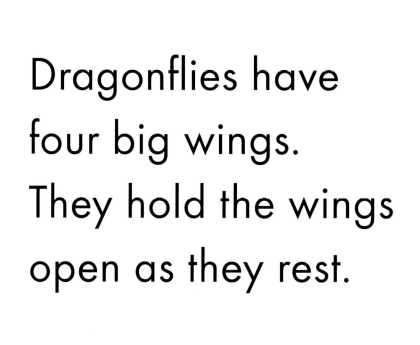

Dragonflies have
four big wings.
They hold the wings
open as they rest.

ACTUAL SIZE:
green darner dragonfly

wing

Dragonflies have huge eyes. They can see in almost every direction!

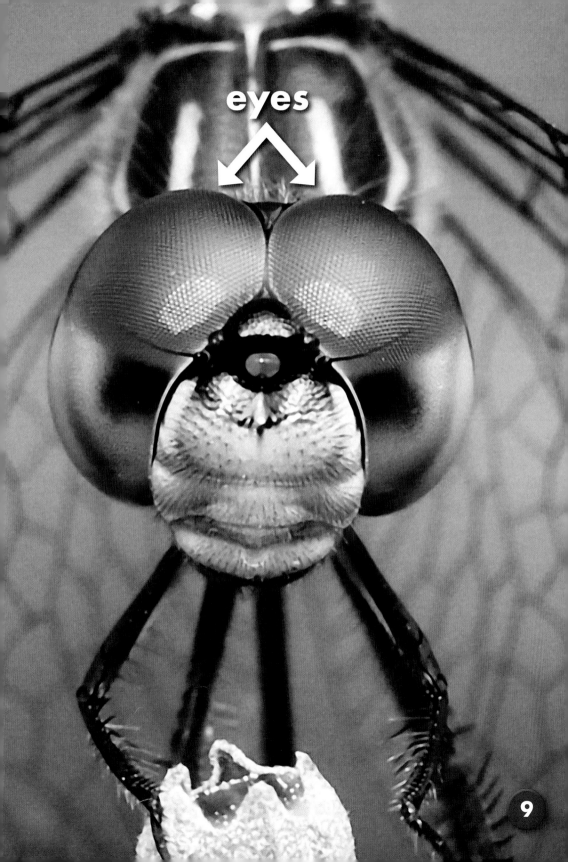

eyes

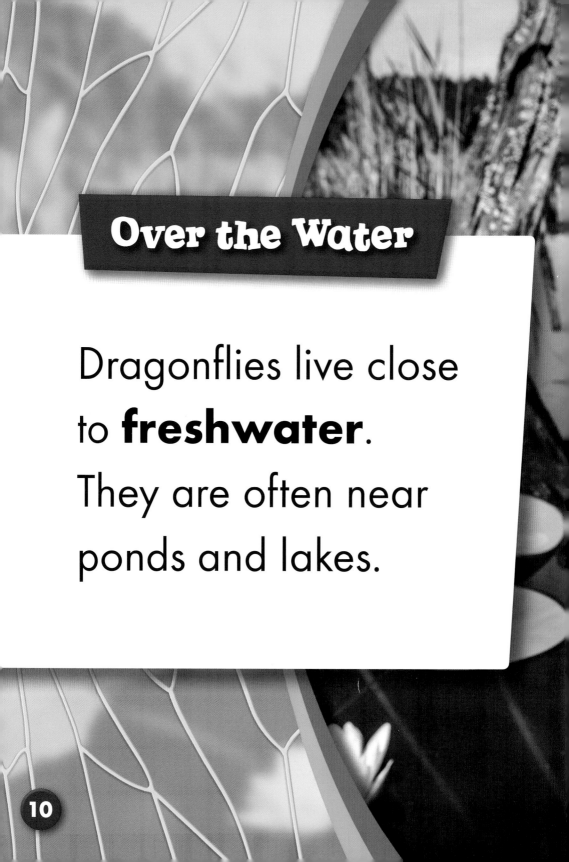

Over the Water

Dragonflies live close to **freshwater**. They are often near ponds and lakes.

freshwater

Dragonflies have to be quick. Adults catch their **prey** in midair!

FAVORITE FOOD:

mosquitoes

Dragonflies lay eggs on water or plants. **Nymphs** then **hatch** from the eggs.

adult laying eggs

eggs

nymph

Dragonflies spend most of their lives as nymphs. They **molt** as they grow.

Nymphs live underwater. They hunt tiny fish and water insects.

DRAGONFLY LIFE SPAN:

1 to 3 years

Dragonflies crawl onto land for their final molt. Then they stretch their wings and take off!

molting

Glossary

freshwater

water that is not salty

nymphs

young insects; nymphs look like small adults without full wings.

hatch

to break out of an egg

prey

animals that are hunted by other animals for food

molt

to shed skin for growth

To Learn More

AT THE LIBRARY

Ipcizade, Catherine. *Dazzling Dragonflies*. North Mankato, Minn.: Capstone Press, 2017.

Statts, Leo. *Dragonflies*. Minneapolis, Minn.: Abdo Zoom, 2017.

Stewart, Melissa. *Zoom in on Dragonflies*. Berkeley Heights, N.J.: Enslow Publishers, 2014.

ON THE WEB

Learning more about dragonflies is as easy as 1, 2, 3.

1. Go to www.factsurfer.com.

2. Enter "dragonflies" into the search box.

3. Click the "Surf" button and you will see a list of related web sites.

With factsurfer.com, finding more information is just a click away.

Index